PORTRAIT OF THE
SOMERSET COAST

NEVILLE STANIKK

HALSGROVE

First published in Great Britain in 2010

Copyright © Neville Stanikk 2010

British Library Cataloguing-in-Publication Data
A CIP record for this title is available from the British Library

ISBN 978 0 85704 006 0

HALSGROVE
Halsgrove House,
Ryelands Industrial Estate,
Bagley Road, Wellington, Somerset TA21 9PZ
Tel: 01823 653777   Fax: 01823 216796
email: sales@halsgrove.com

Part of the Halsgrove group of companies
Information on all Halsgrove titles is available at: www.halsgrove.com

Printed and bound in China by Toppan Leefung Printing Ltd

Title page: Hollerday Hill and Lynmouth from Countisbury Hill, North Devon. Not in Somerset but this would have
to be your starting point as you headed towards County Gate where Somerset, and its coast, starts.

Culbone Cliffs with Exmoor behind. The only real way to see this stretch of coastline is to walk the South West Coast Path.

Sheep grazing on Porlock Common.

INTRODUCTION

My mother had three places that, to her, represented the Ends of the Earth – Rhyll, Goole and Watchet – and, as I never went to any of them until recently, I unconsciously took this definition on board. Now Rhyll really is an End of the Earth, and I've never been to Goole so I can't comment. When I first visited Watchet I had already dismissed it but, against my completely unreasonable expectations, (my mother had never actually *been* there) I actually found it fascinating and, standing on the harbour wall, looking towards Hinkley Point, I couldn't fail to spot that, despite the South West Coast Path ending at Minehead, there *was* a coastline going east.

That memory of a coastline that looked enticing and interesting stayed with me and a couple of years later I was asked to photograph Clevedon and I found myself standing on Church Hill looking south and wondering where *that* coast went.

I was going to have to go exploring and join the whole thing up. Before I did this, I knew as little as everyone else does about the Somerset coast – Exmoor, Minehead, Weston-super-Mare, nuclear reactors and mud. Go on, ask someone (obviously not a local) and you'll find this is the general view of it.

The sea *is* brown, no doubt of that, and there is mud but, by the time I'd finished this project, those two meagre facts had paled into insignificance.

I found a coast not just full of variety but with a pervading sense of magic, mysticism, and history. Churches, towers, castles and ancient buildings dot the landscape. This coast has attracted many on a spiritual level because of its remoteness but the truth of

3

A snow-covered view from Culbone Hill north across the Bristol Channel.

it being a landscape of the imagination was brought home to me when I encountered the coast between Watchet and Lilstock. If you wanted to design a coast that was as interesting as you could make it, you couldn't do better. Everywhere you look is a picture; every ridge of rock beckons you forward; huge fossils are just lying there; and the coastline itself isn't a jumble – it's comprised of beautifully composed geometric shapes covered in clear intricate patterns. It's not chaotic, it's ordered. And the sheer sense of antiquity there, of walking on a giant fossil, is overwhelming.

This book is in the form of a journey from Lynmouth to Bristol. It's not a straight walk, it's a week's holiday, exploring the beaches at low tide, seeing the views from the hills and the sand dunes, and visiting the towns, villages and old buildings.

Inevitably though, if you go on that journey, you'll then become a disciple for this coast, spending the rest of your life telling people to come and visit this place. "No, honestly," you'll say, "it's brilliant." Tell them not to miss this place or that beach. Oh, and you must go to so-and-so and don't forget that village… and so on.

I have had a fascinating time photographing this coast, this unknown gem, and I hope you get some of the same enjoyment from looking at these images and, more importantly, from actually going there. So, Watchet, not the End of the Earth after all.

Porlock Bay from Dunkery Beacon with Bossington Hill on the right.

A winter's morning on Porlock Common, looking across Porlock Bay to Bossington Hill.

Gibraltar Cottages on Turkey Island at Porlock Weir.

High tide in the creek at Porlock Weir.

Low tide at Porlock Weir with Worthy Wood behind.

Photographs from before the 1990s show the apron of farmland below Porlock reaching right to the pebble ridge but after the ridge was breached, and the area immediately behind it became a saltmarsh, it was designated a Site of Special Scientific Interest.

The main street through Porlock, perhaps the village most famous as harbouring the "person from Porlock" who interrupted Samuel Taylor Coleridge's composition of "Kubla Khan".

Bossington Hill and Selworthy Beacon from Porlock Beach.

Rocks at the end of Porlock Beach at Hurlstone Point.

The eastern end of Porlock Beach and Hurlstone Point with the shell of an old Coastguard station.

Walker atop Hurlstone Point with Culbone
Cliffs seen across Porlock Bay.

Porlock and Porlock Common beyond, with a smattering of snow on the Exmoor heights, from Bossington Hill.

Frost on the gorse of Bossington Hill with Porlock Common and the sweep of Exmoor in the distance.

Looking towards Porlock Common, from Lynch Combe on Bossington Hill.

The village of Allerford with the packhorse bridge cottage on the right, surely one of the
most photographed and modelled cottages in England.

View to Warren Point from Higher Town, Minehead.

Autumn morning at Minehead Harbour.

A winter's morning at Minehead, looking from Warren Point to North Hill.

Sculpture, designed by Sarah Ward, on Minehead seafront marking the beginning of the South West Coast path.

The Skyline Pavilion, covering the entertainment, shopping and restaurant facilities at Butlins, Minehead.

Dunster High Street with the
castle at the far end.

Dunster Castle, ancestral home of the Luttrell family. Given to the National Trust in 1976.

Beach huts and groynes at Dunster Beach.

The West Somerset Railway runs both steam trains and diesels from Minehead to Watchet and then inland to Bishops Lydeard. This view is from the level crossing at Blue Anchor, looking towards Conygar Tower at Dunster.

Looking west across the beach at Blue Anchor.

The tide marker at Blue Anchor.

The aptly named Gray Rock at
Blue Anchor.

Pink gypsum (a form of calcium sulphate), a mineral that occurs plentifully in bands locked in the Triassic rock at Gray Rock. The rockfall here makes possible the finding of dozens of these nuggets.

The harbour at Watchet with an approaching storm behind.

Statue of The Ancient Mariner at Watchet.

"Ah! well a-day ! What evil looks
Had I from old and young!
Instead of the cross, the Albatross
About my neck was hung."

Coleridge is commemorated much around the area (for instance, by the Coleridge Way, a long distance footpath) and although he only spent two years living locally, he did compose his two most famous poems here, "Kubla Khan" and "The Rhyme of the Ancient Mariner".

Harbour light on the breakwater at Watchet.

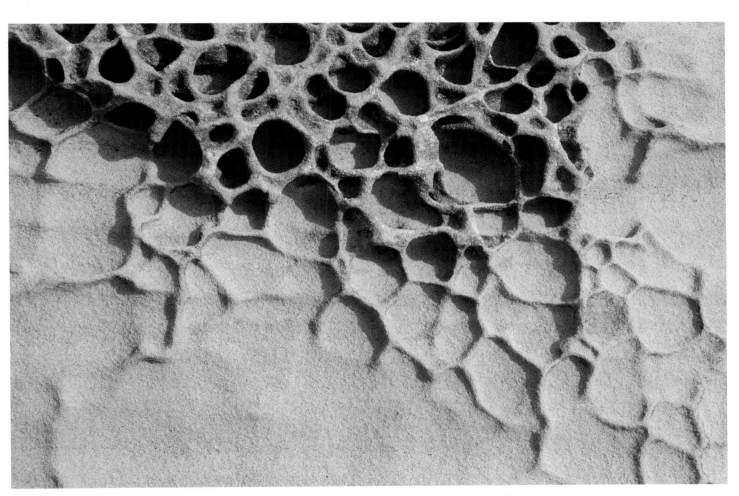

Striking erosion of the breakwater wall stone at Watchet.

Dawn over the limestone ridges at Helwell Bay, Watchet.

Low tide at Splash Point, Watchet.

Part of the Blue Lias limestone pavement at Watchet.

Blue Lias limestone ledges at Splash Point,
Watchet, with Rydon Hill in the distance.

41

Colourful bands of Mercia mudstone on the eastern end of Splash Point, Watchet.

Splash Point, Watchet, seen across the still water of a rockpool at Helwell Bay.

Tilted and eroding limestone at the beach near Doniford.

Limestone ledges above rockpools
at Doniford Beach, with Watchet
in the distance.

Looking towards Watchet and North Hill from Doniford Beach.

Pebbles cover the beach at St Audrie's Bay.

When you encounter the layers of rock, laid down as boldly as this at St Audrie's Bay, and especially level, you can't fail to be impressed by the antiquity of the place, the sense of millions and millions of years.

A wonderful example of natural design,
a limestone pavement at St Audrie's Bay.

Like walking on a huge fossil, ancient pavements of Jurassic limestone at St Audrie's Bay.

St Audrie's Park, a Tudor manor house, refurbished in the 1830s. Probably destined to be many things, as it has already been, down the centuries, it is currently a venue for weddings.

Once part of the village that surrounded St Audrie's Park (originally House), St Audrie's church now sits alone, the village having been cleared and moved in the nineteenth century to allow the owners of the house to have "a more pleasant outlook".

The Chantry Tea Rooms at Kilve. With its unique situation amongst the ruins,
an irresistible spot for a cup of tea in the summer.

The island of Steep Holm in the Bristol Channel, with the South Wales coast behind.
The "rig" is the mobile marine work platform, the Fugro Seacore "Excalibur".

Low tide at Kilve Beach showing the ledges formed by the edges of each Blue Lias limestone layer poking upwards.

As soon as the sea erodes the layers of soft shale beneath the pavements of Blue Lias limestone, squares of it break off and litter the beach, getting rounder with time.

Curving strata of Blue Lias limestone at Kilve Beach.

Overlapping limestone ledges, and rockpool at Kilve.

Alternating bands of shale and limestone in the cliffs at Kilve. As the limestone is eroded, bit by bit, from the cliff, it will form the pebbles on the beach below.

For a photographer (or any sort of artist), the patterns and structure of the rocks along this stretch of coast are a delight. I could easily have spent a week here.

Huge ammonite fossil "negative" at Kilve, ie. the impression that's left, the real thing no doubt carted off long ago.

Edges of the shale at Kilve Beach catch the sunset light.

Blue Lias limestone pavement ledge
surrounded by sand at Kilve Beach.

Sunset-lit cliffs at Kilve reflected perfectly in a pool on the limestone pavement.

Last moments of sunset light on a rockpool at Kilve.

Low tide at Kilve with the ledges and cliffs lit by the sunset twilight.

In a wonderful hilltop situation, St Nicholas' church at Kilton. No longer a parish church but, calling itself a "wayfarer's church", available to anyone who wants to drop by.

Anglers at Lilstock, following the tide across the limestone ledges.

The coastal path at Lilstock with Hinkley Point nuclear power station on the horizon.

The Dunster and Minehead coast from Beacon Hill in the Quantocks.

Staple Plantation from Beacon Hill, looking towards Minehead.

Lichen-covered ammonite in a wall at East Quantoxhead.

The mill pond at East Quantoxhead, with the gates to Court House and the tower of the church of St Mary.

The Gatehouse, an integral part of the ruins of Stogursey Castle, now owned, and rented out as holiday accommodation, by the Landmark Trust. One of the most uniquely situated cottages I have ever seen. Why isn't it nationally famous?

The sea defences at Stolford with Hinkley Point in the distance. The view is of the Hinkley Point B reactor, built in 1967. Hinkley Point A reactor, built in 1957, was closed in 2000 although a new reactor, Hinkley Point C, is planned.

The River Parrett at Combwich Reach,
looking inland.

Old quayside fitting, facing cottages
on Chilton Street, Bridgwater.

Bridgwater Marina. Not on the coast but any trip along the Somerset coast would take you through here.

Beach and sunset at Burnham on Sea, looking towards Steart Island and across Bridgwater Bay.

One of the lakes at Apex Park, Burnham on Sea.

The stone pier at Burnham on Sea. Originally constructed to connect the railway with a steamer to Wales, the old railway lines still lie under the present concrete.

Sea Buckthorn, which grows in profusion on the dunes to the north of Burnham on Sea.

The Pillar Lighthouse in Burnham on Sea,
now a private residence.

The Lighthouse on Legs, at Burnham on Sea, built when it was realised that, despite its height, the Pillar Lighthouse could not be seen from out at sea because of the massive drop in sea level at low tide.

With the Lighthouse on Legs in the background, a remnant of the Second World War coastal defences at Burnham on Sea.

The beach and sea defences at Berrow.

Brean Down, owned by the National Trust, is a limestone outcrop continuing the line of the Mendips.
The same line rises twice in the Bristol Channel as the islands of Steep Holm and Flat Holm.

The cliffs and rock pools of Brean Down from the south.

Previous page: Brean Down reflected in the sand of Berrow Beach.

Cars can be parked on Berrow Beach and, despite warnings, many people forget that the tide really does come in, even though it can go out for a mile and a half, and they find their cars stranded in the sea.

Families walking on Brean Down.

The seaward end of Brean Down, with Brean Down Fort in the distance.

Brean Down Fort, a Palmerston Fort built in the 1860s and closed down in 1900 when a soldier stationed there decided to commit suicide by blowing up the gunpowder magazine. It was refurbished during the Second World War and used for experimental weapons testing and has been owned by the National Trust since 2002.

Outpost of Brean Down Fort, overlooking Howe Rock and the Bristol Channel and the island of Steep Holm.

The eastern end of Brean Down looking across Weston Bay at low tide to Uphill.

View of the marina lake from Uphill Cliff, and across fields to the River Axe.

The "old church of St Nicholas" atop Uphill Cliff.

Uphill Cliff and the old church of St Nicholas with Uphill Marina below, looking out across Weston Bay.

Uphill Marina, with Uphill Cliff behind.

Brean Down and Steep Holm from the beach at Uphill.

Winter sunset behind Brean Down from the beach at Weston-super-Mare.

The beach, and mud beyond, at Uphill.

Pilings on Weston-super-Mare Beach, looking up to houses on Beach Road.

Low tide at Weston-super-Mare, looking towards Anchor Head and Birnbeck Island.

Deckchairs at Weston-super-Mare, looking out to Steep Holm.

The Grand Pier at Weston-super-Mare in 2004, four years before its disastrous fire.

28 July 2008, the Grand Pier burns down. As it happened on a clear summer's day, the smoke plume could be seen for miles, and film of it was shown internationally. Its replacement is due to open in Summer 2010.

Picture courtesy of *Weston Mercury*.

A summer's day on the beach at Weston-super-Mare with Worlebury Hill in the distance.

Traditional donkey and unsure small child on the beach at Weston-super-Mare. The "Weston Eye" can be seen behind – a tourist attraction whilst the pier is rebuilt.

Northern end of the beach at Weston-super-Mare.

Knightstone Island seen at dawn across the Marine Lake at Weston-super-Mare.

Promenade around the end of Knightstone Island.

Looking across the Marine Lake, from the north, towards Knightstone Island.

Rocky beach at Anchor Head, Weston-super-Mare, looking towards Brean Down.

The promenade at Anchor Head, looking out towards Steep Holm.

Birnbeck Pier from Anchor Head.

Birnbeck Pier, Weston's original pier, now derelict and, of course, the subject of endless plans for its renovation. Its dilapidation is so picturesque that every photographer who sees it, wonders just how they could get out to it but there is a *lot* of barbed wire in the way.

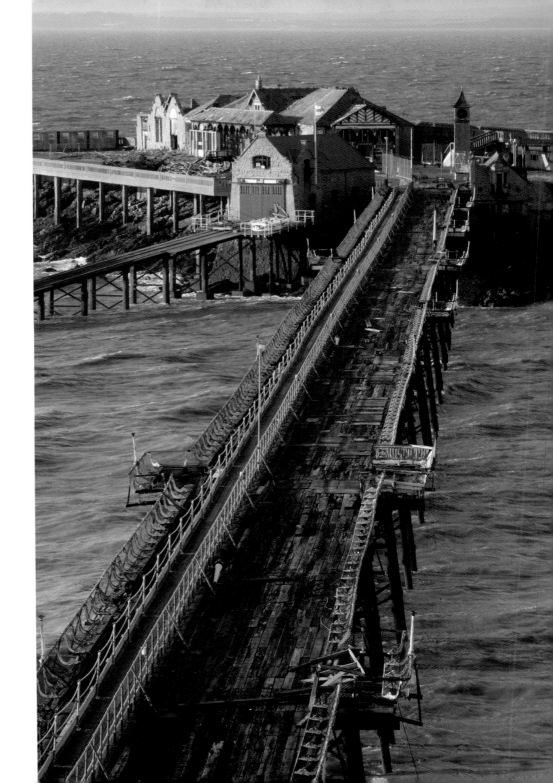

The Monk's Steps, an ancient set of steps leading up Monk's Hill from the church at Kewstoke.

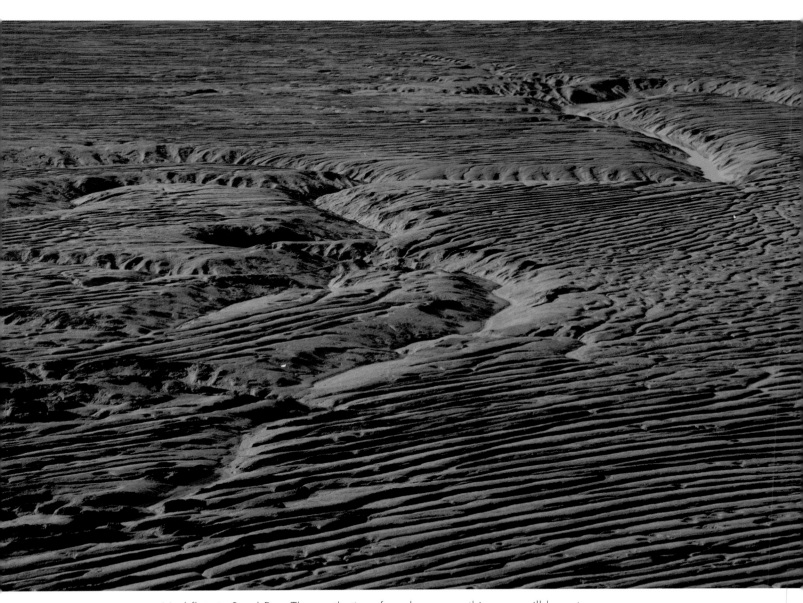

Mud flats in Sand Bay. The aesthetics of mud are something you will have to grapple with if you intend to fully appreciate the Somerset coast.

Exposed limestone on the ridge of Middle Hope (also known as Sand Point), looking out to sea.

Woodspring Priory, now owned and rented out by the Landmark Trust, a former Augustinian priory, founded by Reginald Fitzurse, the grandson of one of the murderers of Thomas Becket, and hence originally dedicated to him.

Small marina in a creek below Wains Hill, Clevedon. The sluice gates are where the
Blind Yeo river (more of a channel really) enters the sea.

The church of St Andrew and its graveyard on the hilltop above West End, Clevedon.

Poet's Walk, a clifftop path over Church Hill and Wains Hill at Clevedon with Sinzel's Lookout on the cliff edge.

Looking towards Church Hill across Salthouse Bay, Clevedon.

The coast at Littleharp Bay, looking towards Clevedon Pier.

Flower bed and promenade
at Littleharp Point, Clevedon.

Clevedon Bay from Littleharp Point.

Houses on Wellington Terrace, looking out over High Cliff, Clevedon.

Clevedon Pier, "the most beautiful pier in England" according to John Betjeman. Opened in 1869 and constructed from Brunel's secondhand railway lines it was almost demolished in 1979 but was ultimately completely restored and re-opened in 1998. A very elegant and atmospheric location.

Clevedon Pier (where you can sponsor a plank with your name on it!) against the late afternoon sun on the waves.

Small lighthouse at Black Nore, Portishead, overlooking the Severn Estuary.

Old red sandstone of the Devonian period at Redcliff Bay, Portishead.

Again at Redcliff Bay, Portishead, old red sandstone with Carboniferous limestone in the cliff behind.

Woodhill Bay, Portishead.

Port Marine, the former Portishead Quays and site of an old power station.

The Angels of Portishead, a sculpture by Rick Kirby, inspired by five radio masts that used to stand on the site. The terrace of Burlington Road is behind.

Opened in 1974, the Avonmouth Bridge is high enough (100 ft) to allow tall ships to reach the Port of Bristol.

The Avon Gorge from the western end
of the Clifton Downs.

The Clifton Suspension Bridge. An icon of Britain, and Victorian engineering, designed by Isambard Kingdom Brunel, weighing 1,500 tons and opened in 1864, it was built despite Brunel's death and a temporary abandonment of the project in 1851 when all the ironwork was sold.

The Clifton Suspension Bridge at night, clearly showing the then-fashionable Egyptian-inspired design of its towers. Sphinxes were intended to top the plinths but they never materialised.

New waterside development on Canon's Road, and Clifton terraces, seen from the Floating Harbour, Bristol. The ship is the *Matthew*, a reconstruction of John Cabot's ship in which he reached Newfoundland and hence discovered North America.

Yacht moored at Prince's Wharf, looking across the Floating Harbour to the Arnolfini Gallery.

St Augustine's Reach, with the Watershed on the left, looking into the heart of Bristol.